RICH AND POOR: EQUALITY AND INEQUALITY

Rich and Poor: Equality and Inequality

Leonardo Polo

Translated by
Roderrick Esclanda
Mark Mannion

Leonardo Polo Institute of Philosophy Press
2017

Cover image:
William Bell, *Iron and Coal*, 1855-1860
National Trust, Wallington, Northumberland

Leonardo Polo Institute of Philosophy
1121 North Notre Dame Ave.
South Bend, IN 46617

www.leonardopoloinstitute.org

Table of Contents

Introduction

Rich and Poor: Equality and Inequality is a short work by Leonardo Polo that examines the commonly held belief that the solution to the problems that arise from poverty and wealth are best solved by equality. In contrast to this widely held view, Polo endeavors to explain how functional inequality is the basis of the family and of society. As he does so, Polo examines the anthropological basis of the family, civil society, and economic systems, as well as notions concerning commutative and distributive justice, business, technology, and communication.

The text of *Rich and Poor* was first published in 1985 by Pablo Ferreiro at the University of Piura (Lima, Peru). It was then republished in 1989 as number 11 of the "Cuadernos del Seminario Permanente Empresa y Humanismo" by the University of Navarra (Spain), and then again in 1990 as part of the book *La vertiente humana del trabajo en la empresa* by Gilder, Llano, Pérez López, and Polo with the publishing house Rialp (Madrid, Spain).

In its most recent form, *Rich and Poor* appears as a chapter of the book *Filosofía y economía* (2012). This book contains other essays by Polo on topics regarding society, economics, and social justice and is divided into three parts. The first part, titled "Anthropological Basis of Economics," contains three lengthy essays that seek to establish the basis of economics on an anthropology of the human person that highlights personal interiority over atomistic individualism. The second part of the book, "Business and Society", consists of five shorter works that study the reality of businesses in connection with the different models of society that have been proposed throughout history, such as liberalism, communism, capitalism, and social-ism. It is in this second part that we find *Rich and Poor*. The third part ("Ethics and Business") consists of six brief articles that deal with ethical themes that should be present in a busi-ness; including, for example, the virtues that should characterize an entrepreneur, the role of governance and obe-dience in a business, etc.

Contents of Rich and Poor

Rich and Poor begins with a consideration of the widespread belief that the solution to the problems that arise from the dis-tinction between rich and poor is to be found in equality. In this type of solution, it is usually implied that there would be neither rich nor poor if there were equality. Polo rejects this solution, and argues that it is based on a mistaken view of work and of the diverse roles played by human persons within society. For him, equality is not a solution to the problem of poverty and wealth because wealth and poverty are not, in re-ality, contrary to each other; rather each has a contrary that is not the other.

Equality is also often linked with justice insofar as it is general-ly assumed that a situation in which some are rich and others are poor is an unjust situation. Polo claims that this is based on the false assumption that wealth and poverty are correlative and opposed to each other. In contrast to this, Polo makes use of a phrase from John Rawls: "only those inequalities that are not advantageous for all is unjust." From this perspective, Po-lo argues that "justice would consist in those inequalities that are advantageous for all, and injustice would consist in those inequalities that are not."

Here it should be pointed out that Polo uses the word "ine-quality" not in the sense that some people have more money or resources than others. Instead, he uses it to describe "dedi-cation to different tasks"; it is "the division of labor or functions that is justified by their complementarity." For Polo, the real distinction between persons in society should not be based on whether or not they are rich or poor, but rather on their functions. For Polo, any type of human society already implies some type of functional inequality according to which the various persons involved contribute to the common good in different ways.

Seen in this way, functional inequality and the division of labor which underpin society arise from human nature; functional equality arises from human relationships, and human relationships arise from functional inequality. Far from being a source of injustice, division of work is a requirement of human nature: "there can be no social man without inequality, because there can be no society without division of labor." And, thus, for Polo, the existence of inequality in society is not necessarily unjust and is, in fact, necessary for the very existence of society. In this context, justice would consist not so much in equality, but rather in a situation in which the functional inequalities (which are dynamic, not static or hypothetical) are to the advantage of all.

The prototypical example that Polo gives to explain his position is the family. In the family, we do not see a number of equal individuals performing the same roles; rather, in order for the family to succeed (which is the same as for it to be a real family), we find that the different members of the family have to play different roles, and that all these need to contribute to the common good of the family. In other words, the family can exist only if there is a division of labor among the different persons that make up the family, and this division of labor means that there is a difference or inequality in work. Thus, for example, the father's activities center on providing for his family, and this makes it possible for the mother to dedicate herself directly to the care of the children. This is in turn necessary because the human child requires a prolonged period of time for development before she is physically and socially viable.

Here, it is important to underline once again that when Polo speaks of inequality, he is not referring to economic inequality or to a situation in which one member of the family wields oppressive power over another. Rather, inequality in this context simply means difference in work and roles. This is clearly seen in the family, where the mother's work is different from that of the father's, but without one being superior or inferior to the other.

With his insistence on functional inequality as natural and required by society, Polo views equality as a notion that derives from both radical individualism and collectivism. This is because both view man as an atomic "individual," who is at times treated as separated from other individuals because of his own interests, and, at other times, as united to others by some type of extrinsic bond. However, according to Polo, both ignore the reality of the human *person*. For Polo, the person is natively *co-existential*. It is from the person that the family arises, and from the family *society*.

From this perspective, Polo sees poverty not as being caused by inequality, but rather as stemming from the "non-utilization of one's own energies," which involves the "unemployment of human capabilities." Egalitarianism is thus unjust because it stifles the development of different human capabilities.

After some considerations about how the family structure is linked with the process of hominization (the evolutionary path that led to *homo sapiens*), Polo extends the notion of functional inequality from the family to civil and economic society. Human progress and civil society, which presuppose a more specialized dedication of the adult members of society, require this projection of the division of labor into associations that are broader than the family. Thus, here too we find division of labor, but with an even greater complexity than in the family.

Because of this increased complexity, the division of labor in society can become problematic. Polo does recognize that in some circumstances inequalities can become injustices, and this happens when the inequalities are not advantageous for all, as when the division of labor is not accompanied by collaboration. The path, therefore, for ensuring that inequalities do not give rise to injustices is to discover how this collaboration can best be achieved. In other words, the division of labor in society has to be organized in such a way that the unity of ends is maintained. If it is not maintained, then the specialization of work produces the opposition of different human groups (or classes) that are pitted against each other, and this gives rise to social division.

As a projection of the division of labor of the family that entails specializations, civil society requires *trade*. Without trade, the specialized division of labor in society is not possible. This is because without trade, the surpluses that the social division of labor gives rise to would not make sense. If the surpluses that a specialized agent produces (precisely because of his specializing in it) cannot be exchanged with the surpluses of another specialized agent, then the division of labor into specializations would be useless.

While it is true that trade is necessary for a society that involves a complex division of labor, Polo considers that it would be a mistake to think that the collaboration of these specialized agents consists solely or principally in trade, and maintains that the essence of the social connections between specialized producers goes beyond commerce. Furthermore, commutative justice, insofar as it establishes equality in trade (receiving equal value for what one gives), does not adequately ensure social cooperation either.

In contrast to this, Polo sees justice as consisting more in the just exercise of human capabilities, and a primary condition for this is that these capabilities not be left untapped. Thus, aside from commutative justice, Polo makes reference to another type of justice, namely, distributive justice. In distributive justice, the person destines her efforts to her most proper end, to what justifies her activities. Distributive justice is the fulfillment of one's own job, which is taken up as a task that has been entrusted to oneself, and is identified with one's capability. In his *Ethics*, Polo describes distributive justice as "to give to each one according to their aptitudes," that is "to give to each one the task that she can best fulfill." For Polo, it is distributive justice that guarantees that the interplay of human endeavors in society is a good for all involved (in other words, a common good).

Polo's emphasis on the role of functional inequality contrasts with what is found in individualism and collectivism, both of which, according to Polo, are based on a consideration of man as an isolated individual. Polo's treatment of division of labor as arising from the very nature of man also contrasts with the Marxist view that division of labor comes about within history and is destined to disappear at the end of history with a classless society.

Polo's understanding of the human person and of the organization of society has a number of practical consequences. For example, with regard to economic activity, it is Polo's view that it is distributive justice that impels the businessman to be daring, to take risks. This leads the businessman to produce and offer products even before there is a guaranteed buyer for them. Thus, according to distributive justice, the key factor in the economy is supply, not demand. It therefore follows that the economy is activated first by the businessman's initiative, by his desire to offer the fruit of his work to others. For Polo, every human initiative is, at its heart, an initiative of giving. This contrasts with the Keynesian approach according to which it is demand that must be fostered first so as to minimize the risk for the suppliers and thus to encourage them to produce.

If one accepts the view that society arises more from human giving than from receiving, and that supply comes before demand, then a social connective other than trade can be discovered. This social connective flows from the human person as giving, and is made manifest in technology.

Polo describes *technology* as "human making that transforms matter." Technology involves practical activity that produces *means*. What characterizes means is that they are useful, and they are useful if there are other means. Nothing is useful by itself; rather, means are useful in connection with that for which it is useful. An instrument always points to another; an isolated instrument is impossible, it is not an instrument at all.

This understanding of a means lies in its use—if one does not know how to use it, then the means is reduced to something for show. In other words, the means are means if they are *available*. Insofar as they are available, the means are can be organized by man's practical conduct. Means therefore has to do with division of labor and sustains trade. The *division of labor* makes sense only if what one produces has a *medial interconnection* with what others produce, and human production is thus characterized by this interdependence.

In this light, division of labor can be seen as a *differentiation in the production of means that refer to one another*. For example, hammers make reference to nails, and nails imply something that needs to be put together with nails, like pieces of wood for a table. Following Heidegger, Polo calls the connection of things that are capable of use a *plexus*.

But where do means come from? According to Polo, means are originally rational human contributions, and this connects with Polo's view that the person is first of all giving, and with the importance that he gives to supply over demand in the economy.

Polo's understanding of this instrumental plexus of means also has consequences with regard to the education and communication that is needed to sustain society. Insofar as use of the means requires a proper understanding of them as means, a person can interact within the instrumental plexus only if she understands the means; otherwise she is excluded from the social relationships that are constituted by this plexus. On the other hand, when persons understand the means, they are able to participate by supplying or contributing new means within the plexus. Moreover, civil society functions well and grows to the same extent that a healthy number of human beings understand the means that form a plexus.

For Polo, the general social connective that makes the means understandable in its connection is *communication*. And, from this point of view, Polo sees that the value of information technology for the strengthening of a new society that is more human lies in its capacity to increase communication and the understanding of practical relationships. Polo then ends his essay with the observation that the increased communication that information technology promises is especially needed in today's complex instrumental plexus, which arises from ever more specialized knowledge and division of labor.

Rich and Poor and Polo's other works

At the beginning of *Rich and Poor*, Polo states that he wishes to examine the proposal that considers equality as the solution to the problems that arise from there being rich and poor in society. He, however, quickly points out that this is an error that it is based on mistaken assumptions about the human person and society. Polo then puts forward his own understanding of society as articulated by functional inequalities and division of labor, both of which, in turn, arise from an understanding of the human person as giving. Throughout his discussion of society and the economy, Polo touches upon a number of topics related with human action such as the family, society, the process of hominization, division of labor, the instrumental plexus, the economy, the role of businessmen, and education. Although it may seem that these are separate and almost isolated considerations that are often times mentioned in passing, they, in fact, all form part of Polo's overall philosophical anthropology. More concretely, the areas mentioned above all form part of what Polo calls the *human essence*, which he also, more technically, calls *availing-of*. The different aspects of human essence (including more detailed discussion of points that are mentioned, but not developed in *Rich and Poor*) are presented in a systematic and orderly manner in his works *Who Is Man?* and *Ethics*, and applications of these aspects to the areas of political philosophy, culture, and education can be found in the essays that make up the works *Philosophy and Economics* and

Helping to Grow. A deeper, more technical study of the structure of the human essence can be found in *The Essence of Man*. And, finally, insofar as Polo considers human essence as the manifestation of the human person, the study of human essence can be followed by Polo's study of the human person as *additionally*, and as gifting in his works *Transcendental Anthropology I* and *Transcendental Anthropology II*.

Mark Mannion and Roderrick Esclanda
Valparaiso, Indiana
November 2, 2017

Rich and Poor. Equality and Inequality.

Leonardo Polo

The Human Family

The subtitle of this conference follows from the fact that wealth and poverty are usually taken as correlative opposed concepts. According to this way of looking at things, and given a level of resources that is not excessively low, there would be neither rich nor poor if everyone had the same amount. Seen in this way, the solution to the problems that come with the distinction between wealth and poverty is equality. But, as the title of a Spanish comedy says, perhaps it would be better that there be "neither poor nor rich, but just the opposite". Now, in order to achieve this objective (for the moment, paradoxical), equality is useless. In other words, the thesis that I am going to hold is this: equality is not a solution to the problem of poverty because neither is it the solution to the problem that wealth poses; both problems must be solved at the together and comprehensively, while at the same time keeping in mind that wealth and poverty are not opposites, but rather that each has a contrary that is not the other.

The clarification of the thesis that I have just stated is the task of this first section; some of the consequences that follow from it are presented in the sections that follow.

The task becomes more difficult when justice enters into the picture: that there are rich and poor is considered as not being just. Naturally, the poor would be those who suffer this injustice. For some, this takes the form of oppression, of dispossession or expropriation; this is the Marxist complaint. On the other hand, others argue that the poor are poor through their own fault; this is the liberal accusation: the poor person is the lazy person. Laziness is a very serious vice that is at odds with industriousness, with the austere, diligent, vigilant application of human capability that is disillusioned with the

1

wiles of this world and is determined to dominate it. As is well known, Max Weber argues that capitalism derives from the Calvinist spirit. Success in this world is a guarantee of success in the next, and is linked to effort and to contempt for mere sensual survival (to which, in contrast, poverty—the form of injustice that is based on inertia that lacks ambition—succumbs). For this reason, becoming rich is taken as a sign of predestination. Some present day theologians have turned this approach on its head, and argue that the rich are practically condemned, because the kingdom of God is reserved for the poor. This is the so-called total option for the poor. But it involves some very specific poor, who are entangled in a task of self-redemption that is quite similar in its intention to the Calvinist one.

In sum, poverty and wealth have to do with injustice insofar as being poor is unjust—either through one's own fault (the Calvinist position and, secondarily, the liberal one) or through the fault of structures imposed by the producers of injustice: those who are already rich (the supposedly contrary position).

It is clear that social ideologies, including the concerns of certain theologians, view the problem of poverty and wealth from a common perspective—they take the two terms to be correlative. This point of view is superficial. We will realize this if we consider the following statement: only those inequalities that are not advantageous for all are unjust. This is an expression from Rawls, one of the theoreticians of today's socialist orientation towards individualism. As is well known, liberalism has made a comeback, above all because it has correctly drawn attention to a number of practical dysfunctions that are inherent to socialism. Rawls' formulation seems to describe an optimal situation in Pareto's sense, because he ponders a situation that is such that its modification would not be advantageous for all. From this perspective, justice would consist in those inequalities that are advantageous for all, and injustice would consist in those inequalities that are not. Thus, the appearance of correlation is broken and is replaced by a holistic consideration that is primary and upon which the correlation, whose meaning is homeostatic, depends.

The difficulty with the aforementioned formula is this: the "for all", that is, its holistic significance, is static (this is also Paretian). The optimal situation is a hypothetical one (for this reason it is not possible to truly dismiss the idea that in a real situation a change that is advantageous only for a few and not for others might not be preferable). But, in any case, it has the merit of highlighting a certain fact, that is, that functional inequality is in accordance with human nature. If the heart of poverty lies in the non-utilization of one's energies, if it consists in the unemployment of human capabilities, then equality is a mistaken objective. One does not necessarily have to be a liberal to see this: the just exercise of human capabilities has as a primary condition that these capabilities be utilized thoroughly, that they not be left untapped. Therefore, it is also clear that seeking functional equality impoverishes (it is unjust). To be equal we would have to reduce ourselves to isolated atoms, to pure individuals; in that case, each one is a non-perfectible whole. Radical individualism is radical egalitarianism; and the opposite: radical egalitarianism cannot be maintained except in the form of radical individualism. But the strict individualistic thesis disregards the development of human capabilities and constructs an imaginary type that substitutes the real man. The image of the solitary perfect man is false in every way. First, because it is not true that human individuals exist completely isolated. Second, because, for man, being alone is evil, it is the most impoverishing of situations that can befall him. The figure of Robinson Crusoe is a fiction. Moreover, Robinson Crusoe presupposes a previous social life.

Inequality arises from human relationships, and also the other way around. In its most elemental form, human inequality is functional. In practice, man is social in terms of division of labor.

This is not a question of a hypothetical situation. It simply means that man projects himself socially in distinct functions.

3

The human social condition and inequality are the same thing: there can be no social man without inequality, because there can be no society without division of labor (another question is that of remuneration; I repeat: this is another matter). If distinction is found at the very heart of man's social character and if this character is natural, then this proves the thesis that inequality is advantageous for all precisely in dynamic terms (not in homeostatic terms, nor as hypothesis); or rather that it is possible to formulate an optimal dynamic in accordance with which the expression "neither poor nor rich, but rather the contrary" ceases to be a paradox.

At the same time, equality is equivalent to radical individualism, which corresponds, as is obvious, with radical collectivism. The uniform collective consideration of society and the consideration of each man as an isolated individual need each other. This is the famous individual-State binomial, the basis of which is the theory of the contractual origin of society. This theory is simply wrong. Man is social by nature. Without society there is no possibility of a contractual bond.

It is now time to show that the division of labor is as primary as society itself, that is, that there can be no society without division of labor; or rather, that the division of labor does not historically come about from a previous social situation in which it did not exist. For this very reason, the division of labor is not destined to disappear at some type of culmination of history. Against fanciful conjectures regarding the origin of society and against the unreality of utopia, it has to be maintained that the division of labor is not a historical phase that is preceded or followed by other phases in which it is not present, and that any weakening of it, instead of leading humanity to greater heights, weakens the exercise of its capabilities.

To focus the question, I am going will refer to Marx. Marx argues that the origin of the division of labor does not coincide with that of human society, but rather that it comes about within history. On this point he accepts a few ideas from a cultural anthropologist named Lewis H. Morgan. According to Morgan, during its first phase, human society took the form of a horde: promiscuity, children in common, structural lability, settlements and technology, dispersed groupings[1]. This would be the primitive situation, and it would only be through the course of the consolidation of transactions and in accordance with an evolution of the relationships of production that the division of labor would appear and progressively grow complicated. Such an explanation is very simplistic. Today's approach to the problem pays special attention to the difference of man with respect to primates. From the evolutionist point of view, what has to be explained is the difference between the process of hominization and the process that comes to rest in the higher primates or that leads to simians. Now, the difference lies in monogamy; that is, in the appearance of the family, in the stabilization of bonds between a male and a female around the care of the offspring. Clearly, the stability of the family nexus is not a horde. The horde is precisely the way of grouping of apes, which is incompatible with the process of hominization.

Thus, the monogamous family and hominization are closely connected with each other. The family society is not only natural to man, but also without it man cannot come to exist. A certain form of society is linked to the origin of the human phenomenon itself: on the one hand, it must be said that man constitutes the family from his humanity (it is a relationship of cause and effect); on the other hand, if the family is not constituted, then a primate does not attain to being man (it is a structural relationship). Obviously, this approach reinforces what the Catholic Church has always held—namely that the family is the basic social institution, that it is of natural law and that marriage is monogamous. It is also clear that the organization of the family gives rise to the division of labor in its most primary form.

---

[1] cf. L. H. Morgan, *Systems of Consanguinity and Affinity of the Human Family* (1871).

Some American biologists[2] argue that the reproduction of primates can follow two strategies: one that approximates what they call strategy R[3]. The other is called strategy K[4]. The strategy close to R is predominant in primates that continue as simians; strategy K is the one that leads to hominization. Strategy R is characterized by the absence of a stable relationship between the male and the female; that is, by the non-existence of the family. This is the horde (or a school of fish). In contrast, strategy K is based on the stability of family relationships. As I have already pointed out, these biologists do not construct an argument with the categories of cause and effect, but rather, an argument of a systematic type; that is, they formulate a central idea that very powerfully coordinates the data. For example, the differentiation between the functions of the lower and upper extremities (bipedalism) is evolutionarily only explicable in primates that are connected with the function of being the nutritional agent of the offspring, which in turn implies that the female dedicates herself to the immediate care of the offspring. That is, when the male plays the role of gatherer, he adopts the bipedal position and does so for a very simple reason: he needs hands to gather and to bring food to his family. This stable dedication of the male to satisfying the needs of the family group brings monogamy with it. If this were not so (strategy R), then the female would have no choice but to search for food for herself and for her child, who would have to accompany her during her more or less arboreal forays. The knocks that this moving about entails would produce irreparable brain damage in the child (strictly speaking, it is incompatible with the human infant cranium and, therefore, also with its brain development), and would

---

[2] The overall meaning of the question can be seen in C. Owen Lovejoy, "The Origin of Man" in *Science* 211, pp. 341-350. Richard Passingham developed field research among apes from this idea.

[3] Care for the offspring is lacking. The success of the species is statistically entrusted to the number of embryos.

[4] Care for the offspring predominates. Ethnologists call this *nesting*.

require a reflexive capability of clinging onto the mother's hairy body (traits absent in the human species). Under these conditions, bipedalism, which is an anatomical fact that is fundamental for hominization, is irrelevant or impossible. So is prolonged human growth. Man needs a long period of time before he is able to fend for himself, which, on the other hand, makes cumulative learning possible. Progress is closely related with the care for children, because the acquisition of culture is only possible in a being that requires many years of living outside of the womb before it is capable of fending for itself. In the biological presentation of this idea, there are many aspects (for example, human sexual dimorphism, etc.) that I will omit. All these can be associated with monogamy as ordered toward the procreation and the education of children.

With this, the Morgan-Marx position is refuted (from a perspective that is also evolutionist), since it is not possible to argue that man comes to be a man if he conducts himself socially like an ape.

The family can be defined as the social form inherent to hominization. The primary division of labor is the dynamic consequence of the family structure. The family develops functions of collaboration that are distinguished from each other by virtue of a sub-situation, which is human infancy. This sub-situation calls for care and formation: it is an ascending temporal vector that distinguishes the functions of collaboration between the father and the mother according to a criterion of proximity. The more proximate caring function is, for this very reason, unable to obtain the resources needed for subsistence, and is possible only if the other member takes care of it. Therefore, to say that monogamous marriage is the basic structure of society inherent in hominization is the same as saying that division of labor is natural to the social man.

This does not exclude other types of human conduct that approximate strategy R, but it is precisely these types that arise throughout the course of history, not at its beginning.

7

Summarizing what has been said so far, if what biologists call the process of hominization is inseparable from strategy K (from the philosopher's point of view, strategy K is not a sufficient – ontological explanation of man; it entails a correlation that clarifies the process within which the direct intervention of God creates the human soul. Taking evolution as a given, it does not seem that the creation of the soul influences the ape's strategy), it is also clear that the division of labor is linked to man since his origin. What is important is that two clearly different ways of living together can be described with sufficient detail: one way of living together that, as we have shown, leads to simians; the other way of living which is proper to man (or hominizising).

From the point of view of wealth and poverty—which is what interests us here—, it should be observed that within the functional inequality of the family, everyone is poor and everyone is rich. The wife, who dedicates herself to caring for the child without taking part in the husband's task of foraging, depends on him in the sense that she cannot fulfill her function if he does not fulfill his. But, on the other hand, the husband would not be able to work if he had not been educated in such a way that he acquired some practical knowledge. *Homo faber* could not have arisen without his having been the object of this care during his infancy, which coincides with a cerebral hyperformalization (which is impossible in the case of the female's arboreal and gathering behavior and without the differentiation of hands). The mother's dedication is, therefore, a factor that is required for man's maturing. It is evident that the child depends on its mother, and that the mother and the child depend on the father; but this dependence, on the other hand, puts the father completely at their service. It is also clear that with the passage of years, the father comes to be dependent (the elderly father will have to be cared for by the child who has become an adult), which shows that the relationship between generations is established in the form of exchanges of dependency that in no way signify a rupture of communication, of collaboration.

One now understands that the injustice that consists in those inequalities that are not advantageous for all appears when the inequalities that are advantageous for all are forgotten or misused; here "for all" indicates that they are advantageous for man as such. If the basic structure of the division of labor is maintained, man can progress without there being rich or poor, but rather quite the opposite. If the functions of collaboration that imply dependency and, therefore, inequality, are destroyed, then the family is destroyed.

The valuation of these relationships of dependency and of collaboration as offensive or harmful stems from individualism's yearning for autonomy. According to this yearning everyone should be self-sufficient. But a self-sufficient husband is an individual who thinks that the mother and the child are provided for by the State or a welfare institution, not by him, because he goes about doing his own things. If, in turn, the wife also wants to be self-sufficient, she neglects her children. And if the child is also seen as self-sufficient, he becomes isolated from his parents. The result is an approximation to the horde: conjugal separation, the collapse of parent-children relationships, protesting bands of children, etc.

These things have recently been happening because of the intrusion of criteria of functional equality that are prevalent in civil society into the realm of the family. The perception of the communitarian value of the distinction of functions lived as collaboration has been weakened; today, it is more its aspect of dependency that is perceived. But if one begins with the fragmentation of interests, then dependency is a negative factor and the different activities are threatened by the denial of cooperation. The more intense the interdependency, the greater this threat is. As far as family is concerned, it is wrong that the husband or the wife fail to look after their tasks (divorce, abortion, etc. is wrong). But the deepest deceit is the self-sufficiency of the young person: if it is generalized, then a descent of civilization and of culture is inexorably produced. A self-sufficient child is a temporal vector of nullified growth. This nullification leaves behind an idle youth, who drift

9

through life, and who resist moral and intellectual disciple, and whose psychological characteristics, centered around a massive affectivity, give rise to groupings that are devoid of humanizing strategy.

From Family to Civil Society

Having established the thesis concerning the irrelevance of equality with regard to the solution to the problems posed by wealth and poverty, we must now turn from the realm of the family to that of civil and economic society, which is broader than the family. Here also we find division of labor, and with an even greater complexity than in the family. Nevertheless, the family is the fundamental society, for which reason the child's growth, the mother's care, and the gathering of resources that is the father's responsibility are basic functions.

This is also how Gilder's book, *Wealth and Poverty*, views it. The author seems to be in agreement with biologists who consider the family as an evolutionary strategy, even though the book deals with the question on different level. When determining the causes of poverty among blacks in the United States, Gilder points out that this occurs in those income levels in which family aid is more than competitive with work. At these levels, African American men work with less enthusiasm than whites, which "is a reflection not of indolence but of singleness. These men lack the motivation conferred by familial demands and the strength imparted by marital support." "Families headed by women are common among the black poor." Therefore, it is argued that "the best way to help black children is to help their mothers (...) it is held that black women suffer from double discrimination, both racist and sexist. (...) As long as this argument prevails, black poverty will inevitably persist..." Even feminist sociologists agree that the effect of independence that is produced by the high income of women is an important cause of family rupture among men of all races and levels of education. Psychologists point out that the father is indispensable for the child's education because paternal education is innovative: when a mother cares for the child she does not play with him, but the father does. Play is a way of posing problems to which the child responds with initiative. Gilder continues by stating that it is important to keep aggressiveness, competitiveness, and man's desire to succeed more in mind. "These qualities have always been the chief assets of lower-class men as they contest for advancement." The attempt, on the part of social institutions, to solve the problems of nourishment, of providing aid for women supplants the father's role. The correlations are very clear: the woman becomes independent of the man when she has no need of him with regard to subsistence, and this happens, in overall terms, especially in the lower classes, when there are subsidies. Subsidies are a way of spreading social equality, of correcting the injustices that are produced by shortages; but, in the long run, it does not solve the problem, but rather makes it worse.

In sum, progress is linked with maintaining the family structure intact. One way of undermining it is to seek to supplant the husband's function as provider, and not because women work, but through subsidies; that is, by state supplanting, which is, in turn, based on an egalitarian ideology. But in the end, this way of proceeding does not solve anything; rather, it condemns the poor to always be poor. This idea from Gilder is proof to the contrary that the family society implies the division of labor. Since the family is a natural and primary social institution, state intervention is arbitrary and artificial. With it family crisis and impoverishment are fostered. A subsidized poor family—even though it may be uncomfortable to accept it—cannot cease being poor because its functional dynamic is paralyzed when its structure is weakened.

Undoubtedly, inequalities become injustices when they are not advantageous for all. That is, when the necessity of dividing labor is not accompanied by collaboration. It also cannot be denied that the division of labor frequently gives rise to social breakdowns, to divisions. This happens above all in the realm of civil society. Inequality is then seen as lacking justification. However, not even then is functional equality a solution

11

(strictly speaking, neither is it possible). Also, this is when wealth and poverty appear as relative opposites. In a normal family there are neither poor nor rich, but rather quite the contrary, as the title of that work I mentioned says. Neither the wife is rich, nor is the child, nor is the father. But, at the same time, no one is poor, but rather all collaborate.

Therefore, the correct thing to do is to maintain the following. First, that the division of labor is required by humanity since its origin and in its historical progress. Second, that its justification is found in coordination and in collaboration. Third, that the division of labor, whose first setting is the family, extends from there to civil society. Fourth, that through this extension it can become problematic. Fifth, that this problematic character suggests egalitarianism as a solution. Now, if egalitarianism is introduced into the family, it destroys it. Sixth, consequently it is wiser to work out how it would be possible to achieve collaboration in the extension of the division of labor to civil society instead of seeking to implant a homogeneity that is illusory and anti-functional, especially on the basic level of the family. It must especially be kept in mind that the crisis of the parents' educating function gives rise to youth who have no drive, and, therefore, to a foreseeable degradation of the future.

Thus, the issue that we are going to deal with is the following: in what way can social relationships in general be based on cooperation? The difficulty of the matter lies in that, although the family is the primary form of society, the division of labor in civil society seems to be of a different nature: its subjects are, usually, the providing agents of the family. Therefore, in principle, these relationships seem to require the existence of correlative surpluses and shortages; that is, an arrangement for exchanging products in which associations barely count. But in the exchange of things the criteria for justice is equality— commutative justice—. Moreover, trade is not a collaboration, a pooling together, but rather a formally transitive operation consummated in its very reciprocity, a compensated combination in homeostatic form whose connective is money. From this comes the distinction between exchange value and use value: the use is external to exchange, which, in turn, is consolidated by virtue of price. It is clear, on the other hand, that the division of labor in civil society gives rise to associations that group together those who are specialized in similar tasks (for example, unions). But these associations do not ensure collaboration, since they concern themselves with the protection of interests or of acquired privileges.

Collaborative relationships, whose prototype is the family, has to be sought out by studying the central role that communication has in human society. Language, not money, is the social connective that ensures that the division of labor does not lead to division among human beings.

Questions

— Wealth and poverty depend on unequal wages, which can and, at times, should be reviewed.

A: I am speaking about inequality in its elementary sense, which does not consist in some people making more money and others less (a debatable inequality), but rather in the dedication to different tasks. This inequality is the division of labor or of functions that is justified by their complementarity; moreover, it is required by man's nature, since without division of labor only simians are possible. The inequality that I am referring to contrasts with, for example, the French Revolution's motto (equality, fraternity, liberty). This is an incoherent motto because if there is equality, then there is no fraternity and there is no maternity or paternity, etc. Neither does equality produce liberty, but rather it needs pressure groups in order to maintain itself. Man should not be distinguished into rich and poor, but rather by their functions. If the notion of equality is postulated in general, then inequality appears as something negative, backward. This is false; what is backwards is equality, because equality is atomism.

— Before God all men are equal.

A: This is a different matter. God shows no partiality to persons, but he does judge according to works. We are all children of God and whoever fulfills the functions that we consider more humble might be loved by God more than the one who does other things that are more important from our point of view. For this reason, on another occasion I said that it would be good to "make an ode to a kibble". God uses criteria that are different from ours; we differentiate men by their work and we assume that there are jobs that justify better wages or imply greater social status.

— Could you avoid the word "inequality", which is too controversial and sociologically not very exact, relative.

A: Agreed. I used the word inequality, but we can speak of differences. The term inequality is mathematical, abstract. The division of labor is not inequality of work, but rather difference of work. Is a mother's function inferior to that of the father? No: both are tied together by service to the children.

Commutative and Distributive Justice

The lines that I consider basic for the exposition of wealth and poverty with a view to overcoming the problems that their dialectic correlation pose, are inscribed in human nature itself. It is of natural law that man develops different collaborative activities. Man is naturally social and the division of labor is present in society since its origin. The word "division", like the word "inequality", which I used following Rawls, expresses the distribution of labor as a non-exclusive, but nevertheless predominant assuming of different functions by different agents. As an argument in favor of this approach, I made use of some ideas from evolutionist biologists who seek to explain the process of hominization. The strategy that leads to simians takes no notice of the family and, therefore, of the specialization of functions. In contrast, the humanizing strategy consists, precisely, in that the male takes care of the female and of the offspring and is, in this way, bound to them in a stable manner. This makes it possible to systematically explain a series of anatomical and physiological traits that are proper to man, as well as the possibility of a prolonged process of education that is required after its premature birth. With this, we reject the approach according to which the division of labor is an event that makes its appearance within the course of human history, but not at its beginning. For the same reason, that approach proposes the overcoming of the division of labor as the finality of history, or as the most perfect society.

The attempt to transcend the division of labor is as erroneous as the thesis regarding its origin. Hominization is incompatible with the horde.

Historical progress, in turn, depends on education. The greater the amount of knowledge and the advance of technology, the more time man needs in order to be educated, that is, to arrive at the conditions needed for social viability and effectiveness. Therefore, in the end, historical progress results in continuing and complicating the primordial strategy. The functional differentiation for the sake of the very prolonged educational care of the next generation requires the family institution as its basis.

In that situation, there are neither rich nor poor, but rather quite the contrary. The child is poor in a certain sense; if he is left alone, he dies, etc., because he lacks the capacity to acquire material resources, and his viability is precarious; but this itself is a condition for growing and for attaining a high level of performance through care and education. If the child were already specified, if he were capable of fending for himself soon after being born, then his education would be very limited and progress null; this is what happens in the animal species in which, genetic mutations apart, there is hardly any change. The human species progresses without needing genetic mutations.

Historical progress is a projection of the division of labor unto human associations that are broader than the family, its prolongation in forms that are also more complex and clearer, which presuppose a more specialized dedication on the part of the adult family members. Civil society is also based on division of labor and expresses its prominence.

Marxist analysis is wrong on this point too: it is not true that there is a reduction of classes (if class is understood as a social category that reflects the division of labor—the set of individuals defined by a particular and homogenous function within the structures of production that are present at each historical moment). There is no reduction of classes, nor is there, historically, the extreme opposition between two of them: capitalists and proletarians, after which the society without classes would come. For Marx the classless society transcends the specialization of work (the capitalist class, as a consequence of the contradictions proper to the accumulation of fixed capital, will disappear and will be followed by a generic humanity whose members will not be diversified by their functions and who will be capable of everything). Now, just the opposite happens: as history advances, there are more types of work. Thus, present day society is the setting for an ever greater sectoralization (Helmut Schelsky) in which the attempts at organization according to classes fail; we are in full union crisis, because, for example, it is increasingly difficult to coordinate the interests of workers according to the idea of a unity of class.

Today, this idea has been adopted by many sociologists, even Marxist ones (in the generic sense). Not only has the simplification of society not been produced, but rather, the opposite—its complexification—has come about. The division of labor has not weakened. Grouping work under a common rubric (the proletariat) exclusively in opposition to capitalism entails confusing different types of jobs.

In any case, the expanded projection of specialization outside of the family in what is called civil society brings with it, together with all its advantages, the important problem of

16

collaboration. The division of labor has to be organized in such a way that the unity of ends is maintained; if it is not maintained, the opposition of human groups (call them classes or whatever one wishes) appears: the specialization of work accompanied by social division. Now, if civil society is the expanded projection of division of labor transformed into specialization, then it clearly requires trade. Some thereby conclude that it is the network of trade that is the very structure of society. Likewise, a difference between rich and poor can be produced within the network of trade. If one is given little for what one produces, that is, if the rule of equality that is called commutative justice (the more you give, the more you get; the value of what you give is equal to the value of what you receive) does not hold, then poverty and wealth become correlative situations. For this same reason, it would be important to avoid excessive gain. Commutative justice will have to be ensured in every case and be reestablished every time it is violated.

As I see it, this approach is very shortsighted. That is, if society effectively consists in the relationship between specialized producers or, in other words, if the connective of the social specializations that are superior to those of the family is trade, then seeking that this not give rise to gain and impoverishment (ensuring commutative justice in general) is a vain hope. If we take this approach, then we find ourselves with an unsolvable problem: there will always be rich and poor, and there is no way to avoid it. Why? Because commutative justice in general cannot be established with exactitude. This is very clear: all that is needed is a situation of monopoly, or a greater capacity for resistance on the part of a few, in order to put others in the situation of having to pay what is asked for. But this difficulty is even greater, for which reason trying to remedy it leads to forced measures.

I insist. If the connective element is exclusively trade, then wealth and poverty are inevitable. That situation of the family in which, as we were saying, there are neither rich nor poor, but rather quite the contrary, is transformed into another situation in which there is, necessarily, poor and rich, precisely because of having given everything over to equality in trade. It must now be said that commutative justice is not all of justice. If we entrust everything to it, then we are betting on a complete equality that is illusory: is it true, let us say, that a kilogram of bread is worth a decigram of beef? Is it true that a pack of cigarettes is worth twice a kilo of bread? Who could know this? If someone were to appeal to the criterion of relative scarcity, he would then be referring to a monopoly. But, furthermore, scarcity is very variable, for which reason equality in trade is a question of chance or of cleverness. For example, that someone has had the foresight to stock up on certain goods; he can then delay the sale of his own products and provoke its shortage. Here a clear inequality is noted: favorable opportunities, greater or lesser talent for calculation, etc.

In sum, as I see it, the notion of commutative justice, that is, of equality in giving and receiving things, does not ensure social justice; the exchange of products is very advantageous, but it does not ensure that there will be neither rich nor poor, or that the poor will not always be poor; but rather the opposite: there are so many failures in exchanges, provoked or natural, that the situations of poverty and wealth tend to increase (even though the subjects of one or another situation may change). Adam Smith noted that without trade, the social division of labor is impossible. However, the essence of the social connections between specialized producers goes beyond commerce. If the possibility of establishing a criterion for equality according to commutative justice exists, it is on the level of trade. But there are higher social connections, and also narrower and more intense ones. For this reason, the system of collaboration, the coming together for common ends (it would be good to use the classic expression "common good"), is not limited to commutative justice.

I will attempt to clarify this last assertion. The examination of family relationships brought to light the existence of a division of functions that is at the service of the child. If we apply the Marxist notion of expropriation to family relationships, the result would be that the father is expropriated of what he produces when he gives it up to the other members of the family. Similarly, if the expropriation happens within history, then the there was no family organization at the beginning, and at the end there is the classless society. For this reason, I hold that liberalism and Marxism, individualistic atomism and collectivism, are not antithetical, but rather begin with common assumptions. These assumptions mean an erroneous interpretation of the social nature of man. The error is a cutting back, a limitation that consists of seeing, within the dynamic of human relationships, one sole object which is trade at the service of the needs or of the selfishness of the individual. It is an attempt to make self-sufficiency and the providing of necessities that is achieved at a greater scale with specialization (Marx's polytechnic man presupposes the paralysis of capitalization) compatible.

It is true that without trade the surpluses that the social division of labor gives rise to would not make sense. If whatever extras one has (precisely because one has specialized in producing it) cannot be traded for whatever extras someone else has (who has also specialized) then the division of labor would be useless. But the cooperation of specialized social agents does not consist in trade, and it is an error on Smith's part not to have pointed it out. Without cooperation, selfishness rules and social relationships tend toward being a zero-sum game (in order for some to gain, others must loose). Family relationships are clearly not a zero-sum game. Thus, although the husband turns in all his earnings to his wife for her sustenance and that of their child, this does not mean a loss for him, because in this way he also gains: he gains humanity, he destines his efforts to his most proper end, to what justifies his activities. And this is the deepest justice: not commutative justice, but rather distributive justice.

Fulfilling one's own job as a duty is the basic form of justice. To do what one does, in the way it should be done, and because it should be done, imbues the doing with its primordial justification: the job that is done is a task, the entrusting of which is identified with one's capacity. Taking charge of a task points to the dignity, to the merit by virtue of which the exercise of the activity is neither capricious nor contingent, but rather appropriate, beneficial and unavoidable—due—. Man cannot renounce this facet of his acting.

Thus, it should be said that distributive justice guarantees what is usually called the common good, that is, that the interplay of human endeavors in society be a good for all. This guarantee is deeper than the level of trade and prior to it (it is the intrinsic value of action). Certainly, trade is a condition of possibility for the division of social labor, and it is also true that it implies a mutual advantage (if it were not so in principle, there would be no trade), but it is not the culmination of the social connection. Seeking to solve social problems—for example, the difference between rich and poor—by limiting oneself to ensuring equality (for example, through the redistribution of income), is pure short-sightedness.

Let us see what the politics of the redistribution of income means. Assuming a failure of commutative justice—that is, the enrichment of some and the correlative impoverishment of others—, a separate instance, which would be the State, proceeds with compensation. The compensation is achieved by taking the surplus part of earnings from some and giving it to others. In this way the State sets itself up as a remedy for the lack of justice because it reestablishes social equality. But this way of ensuring social equality makes sense to the same extent that the imbalance of the system of give and take understood as the connective of the division of labor is inevitable. Now, since there are stronger connectives, not all of the problem lies there. Also, the tax burden required by the redistribution increases in such a way that it becomes a detriment to economic activity and intrudes into all social areas. This points to a clear contradiction in the state's attempt to remedy the failures of commutative justice that are seen in the differences of income: on the one hand, the position that makes trade the principal social connective is not abandoned; on the other hand, this connective is substituted and weakened by the politics of re-

20

distribution. There is a temporal alternation: the person who at one moment becomes rich is, at another moment, expropriated of it by the State. This alternation makes sense in some cases or to a certain extent, but is neither useful in all cases nor is it the only measure. Moreover, with this one achieves, at best, a static balance and almost always a regression, because if the relative enriching and impoverishing produced through trade are remedied by an added compensation, the functional regime of society is made more expensive and nothing is added.

The family model is foreign to this type of equilibrium, since it contains a temporal vector of progress that justifies the differentiation of functions: namely, the education of the children. Having children and educating them is to aim for more. In contrast, having recourse to redistribution as compensation for the poor functioning of commutative justice on its own plane requires a complementary factor that is a restraint, and leads to social paralysis. The critique made by the Friedmanites (those liberals who realize that presently there is too much State) is an accurate critique, but it is not accompanied, in the form that they propose, by a satisfactory investigation of those spheres of cooperation that are distinct from pure trade. State interventionism hinders the economy, employs an enormous bureaucracy, is very expensive, and does not attack the problem at its core. In my view, the worst aspect of state interventionism is bureaucracy, the antiquated and ineffective system of control. If the human nervous system, which controls the organism, functioned like a bureaucracy, it would spend a large part of the energy that man procures on nourishing itself, and it would be dysfunctional for the body; precisely, the value of a system of control is inseparable from the energy that it expends. Experience shows that insisting on resolving the social problem in terms of equality gives rise to very expensive systems of control, which impoverish and ruin the functional basis from which they are nourished. In sum, the socialist model implies an excessive expenditure of unproductive human energy. And since it has to be justified, it multiplies

21

readjustments needlessly, thus introducing confusion into the public conscience.

The liberals' critique of state interventionism is thereby justified from the point of view of effective functioning. Socialism's state bureaucracy is a dead weight. The rise of this model comes from Keynes's theory of general equilibrium. But this is nothing but a certain interpretation of it. The increase of the State's functions, which liberals consider as disruptive of the laws that regulate the market, is a consequence of a social-democratic reading of Keynes that distorts his intention. Keynes's general theory assumes that not everything that is saved is invested, that is, that a large portion of savings is unproductive, or that there is not enough entrepreneurial spirit to guarantee full employment and meet the people's needs. If this is so, then it seems desirable that a greater demand be fostered, which is achieved through the increase of the majority's capacity for spending. Thus, it is a question of incentivizing the productive employment of those savings that are not automatically transformed into investment.

This is the key to Keynes's model, which is very different from the idea of equality: something like a psychology of the rich. Keynes seeks the reactivation of supply starting from the fact that the only possible activator of supply is demand: if we increase the demand, then we favor the supply. When inequalities are produced in trade, demand is an enticement by which a large part of what is accumulated is prevented from being taken away from the economic circuit. Increasing the population's capacity for spending diminishes the tendency toward non-productive hoarding of wealth. The objective is to relaunch the economy toward a high level of equilibrium, while preventing the specialized agents who become rich from leaving the circuit through their purchasing of things that have nothing to do with the continuity of exchanges; for example, antiques. In the final analysis, the State is, for Keynes, a stimulus for the investor, but not directly, but rather by making his task easier. When is it easier? When one can make more; when one make more? When there is more demand.

The correctness of Keynes's insight depends on whether or not it is true that those who are specialized in investment disengage from this very function; that is, if being rich means being a hoarder, which is equivalent to impoverishing the system of trade. But the remedy that is proposed leads to the rise of what we could call businessmen of convenience, not by vocation. This type of people, in which the eagerness for risk is very limited, have been the real promoters of the consumer society. They could also be called spies of the signs of demand (practices of marketing). And it is, in fact, from Keynes's approach that one can tell that the love for risk is almost nonexistent. Since risk does not attract the socialist bureaucracy either, both the Keynesian businessman as well as the social-democratic politician are incapable of promoting human dignity: they are shot through with inauthenticity, their activity is intimately unattended, he pays no heed to distributive justice. Strictly speaking, distributive justice compels one to be daring: in the case of the businessman, to not wait until one has a guaranteed buyer before producing, to trust in supply. According to distributive justice, the key to the economy is supply, not demand. On the contrary, Keynes states that supply does not guarantee demand because man's capacity to supply is very limited, such that if the businessman is not previously presented with demand, if the fear of risk is not eliminated, then it is not possible to achieve activation of the economy. The opposite thesis, which Jean-Baptiste Say had already formulated in the beginning of the 19th century, points to the factor that animates the relationships of trade, to the vigorous connective of the division of labor.

We still have to ask if Keynes is right. If he is, then it must be said that there are poor people because there are few people who are ready to produce, to promote work. The cause of poverty is the lack of initiative, be it private or whatever one wishes; ultimately: human initiative. Let us bring the question to the level of the primitive family: if the gatherer thought "this bunch of bananas is huge and the way home is long; therefore, better to eat them here and carry only a few and not use up my energy", it is evident that the wife and the child would be poorly served. Also, if the male gatherer were that lazy he would end up organizing that equivalent of a horde, which is the gang: the gatherer on strike would go roaming about with others who are as demoralized as he is. That is, strictly speaking, what Keynes says: whoever becomes rich acts like an ape because he stops producing.

Some conclude that in order to avoid similar kinds of behavior, becoming rich should be banned. Others think that these failures can be avoided by increasing the incentives. But these arguments are forced, because they assume that man has no interest in offering the fruit of his work to his fellowmen, or that his natural tendency is gangsterism. With this approach, the meaning of economic life is ruined and the proposed solutions are rendered null and void (the socialist bureaucracy would also be a gang). It has to be proved that Say is correct and Keynes is not.

It is only because our sense of the social bond is not as strong as our sense of the family bond (and it should be, because otherwise the family would dissolve) that we do not risk supply before there is demand. Supply is authentic if it accepts the risk of not being accepted. In accordance with this double acceptance, supply connects with demand. If there are enterprising people, then others grow rich. Or, in more direct terms: that there be neither rich nor poor depends on the entrepreneur. The dearth of entrepreneurial spirit is the relinquishing of the common good (if we do not accept that the common good consists in the primacy of demand, which is Keynes's pessimistic thesis).

Man was made more for giving than for asking. It is true that human nature is wounded with respect to its orientation to the end. The monkey, relates Kipling, is the most despised animal of the jungle because it is the fickle and frivolous animal par excellence. It is not an animal that plays. Play is an activity with rules (at its highest levels play is sapiential); the monkey, on the other hand, when it is not urged on by immediate needs, goes through a series of aborted attempts, it loses itself in incoherent rambling about. Rambling about also characterizes the vital on-goings of the man who is wounded in his capacity for ends, as can be seen in the false social promoters who are rich with yachts, trips to foreign cities, deaf to the official requirements of a bureaucracy that is corrupt and incapable of guaranteeing them investment without risk of loss.

It is clear that Keynesianism presupposes an already mature market, the strengthening of which is a question of degree. If the domestic market is weak, then additional difficulties have to be added that explain, to a large extent, this general feeling of helplessness that leads to the ineffectiveness of those who govern and to the flight of scarce capital that is brought about by the exportation of raw materials. But this itself demands better work, first of all, from whoever is in charge of promoting work, from whoever is supposed to provide it. In this sense, a broad effort at training is needed.

Using, once again, ideas from Gilder, I will try to explain the meaning of risk. Risk does not mean insane daring or political arbitrariness or revolutionary terrorism. It means not accepting the primacy of the market, but rather becoming aware that supply is previous to demand and to be ready to establish a market.

It is apparently frequent in pre-cultures that there is an institution that shows that placing supply before demand is not a modern invention[5]. This consists in that, while counting on his family, an individual busies himself for some time with gathering food. When he has amassed a sufficient amount, he organizes a banquet to which he invites other members of the group. It is understood that this same thing will be done by others; in any case, doing it merits honor and omitting it dis-

---

[5] C. Llano, J. A. Pérez López, G. Gilder, L. Polo, *La vertiente humana del trabajo in la Empresa*, Madrid, Rialp, 1990, p. 99.

qualifies one socially. As can be seen, the institution fulfills a function of supply with the hope of some similar future conduct on the part of the invitees: that is where the risk is. If everyone responds, a great advantage is achieved; that is, the satisfying in a general sense of this need (which is very important and which appears in every culture with variations) for enjoying festive days, for celebrating a situation of prosperity that is shared by giving. It is obvious that the feast must not be confused with partying, which is something superficial; the feast, on the other hand, affirms man in his existence.

Furthermore, this institution, which is the complete opposite of a zero-sum game and which can cancel itself out if too many people who fail (what in Spain we call a "gorrón" [English: a "freeloader"]), is the precursor of the entrepreneur inasmuch as he can be found in a low technology phase.

We can say that the figure of the entrepreneur is already in some way present wherever there is civil society, even though it be very primitive. What brings this about? How do anthropologists explain this figure? Its appearance is not the result of calculated interest, but rather of the desire for honor, of emulation, of everyone wanting the same thing but through success, unlike homogeneous egalitarianism. Strictly speaking, feast time is the highest time, and these men seek it out as they can. F. de Closets notes that the socialist Keynesians have invented the adage "take and you will receive", and live as if it could be made reality. Another phrase says "give and it will be given to you". Within the human order this phrase is not a sure thing. Thus, if there is an abundance of astute people, of individuals who think themselves smart because they live like parasites without suffering any penalty, then the aforementioned phrase fails, and whoever accepts being a supplier has run a risk and has failed. However, every human initiative is, at heart, an initiative of giving: the initiative of receiving is not primary. Having the initiative is the same as giving, and the terminus of the initiative is the same as receiving. Therefore, for the priority of giving over receiving to not take place, it would be necessary that the human conduct directed toward

26

others be only reactive and not a true initiative. But in that case no one would receive anything. Thus, it must be concluded that initiative must be fostered if distributive justice is aspired to. It seems to me that the Hispanic's renunciation of initiative is due, to say it quickly, to the fear of ridicule (of being taken for a ride). The Hispanic is quite convinced that if he takes the initiative to give, he will be made fun of; for this reason, he is little inclined to run the risks of civil life. It can be noted that in the pre-cultural form of gifting, money was not needed because trade was direct and there was no need for a measure of abstract value, which makes comparisons of value among many things (money is the means for generalizing exchanges) possible. With money, the possibility of finding out what the other likes more, or rather, of taking into consideration the preferences of others appears. The primitive supplier cannot make choices because he has few things at his disposal. An important difference between private and state initiative lies in this. State initiative is anonymous and, therefore, subsidies are not given in accordance with personal expectations, but rather as a block. Nor does it measure the needs of each one correctly. In contrast, what we call a gift (for example, a Christmas gift) is a more flexible form of exercising the gifting initiative.

A gift is appreciated both for its economic value as well as for the interest shown to one's own preferences. This example can perhaps help draw attention to the fact that a modern entrepreneur also has the possibility of regulating his supply in accordance with a number of preferences. The entrepreneur does not fulfill this function when he becomes a mass operator. For this reason, the large business resembles the State, and both have in common a large bureaucracy. We once again confirm that the liberalism-socialism opposition is apparent: both begin with a common assumption and both end up with a bureaucratic organization.

The small business is a better alternative. In order to make it into the key of the social dynamic, it is necessary that the objective conditions for ending bureaucracy exist. Putting an end to bureaucracy is equivalent to establishing a horizontal control; not a superimposed control, which separates the initiative of supply from demand and requires the Keynesian stimulus of demand, as well as bureaucratic mediation. Note that the control function is another connective.

What can be done so that the element of control be on the level of supply in such a way that it directly affects trade, and so that social connectives do not multiply due to artificial need? According to some authors, this can be achieved through information technology. This is what, among others, J. Naisbitt proposes. The exercise horizontal social control, which is almost a self-control, consists in taking advantage of the possibilities of information technology. According to Naisbitt, the role of the bank would also thereby be modified. The bank can become another expensive, conservative system of control. It does not seem fitting for financial capitalism to control the industrial entrepreneur, since this control brings with it a subordination that is not all that effective.

In sum, information technology would make possible an extensive reorganization of society with a view to promoting that connective which seeks the common good on the same level as trading. It involves a social formula that is clearly different from bureaucracies. Naturally, information technology can be monopolized by existing control procedures, which would lead to a very serious failure of freedom, even greater than what humanity suffers today. It should not be forgotten that the initiative of giving implies freedom; moreover, man is not, strictly speaking, free until he gives. A freedom that spurns supply is a negative freedom, one that is conditioned by the request for guarantees. Whoever makes uses of his freedom to the full runs the risk of non-correspondence; this is the risk that is specific to the society of free men: the others can prevent the initiative from being reborn in themselves. In the family this is the risk of marriage, of paternity. If it is thought that one must avail of an order (cultural, legal) that, for example, ensures the husband's or the wife's fidelity, then one is looking to reinforce a debilitated freedom. But in the end, conjugal fidelity belongs to each one's initiative. Certainly, infidelity in this order of things is contrary to natural law and the legislative power has no power to sanction it or to legitimize situations opposed to it. But man does not fulfill the natural law like an animal does. A father also has to accept the risk of the non-fulfillment of educative objectives on the part of the child; otherwise, the child would be a mere extension of its parent; to seek this out is paternalism. To be a father is to be an instigator of freedoms.

If risk is inherent to freedom, then the yearning for security implies a loss of freedom. The free man loves risk, not for its own sake (he does not play Russian roulette), but rather because the reward for risk is enormous, and cannot be substituted by automatic successes.

Freedom in time is risky because the gifting initiative requires maturity: it is a growing initiative, which is in no way an inertial prolongation. Here risk appears in the form of choosing between growth and goods that are immediately within reach. For this reason, it is also proper of freedom to play for the long term. Short term objectives are a sign that risk is being avoided. But the value of the objectives are thereby also curtailed. This is clear in the family. Having children becomes a long term investment because in order for the child to be ready to correspond many years are needed.

It seems to me that the key to the problem has been laid out. It is clear that when faced with this approach it is always possible to ask where or with whom to start. In other words, is a gifting activity viable within a social environment that does not know about it, one that is impoverished because of a lack of initiative? That is, the risk seems very apparent when the conditioned reflexes of people are contrary to giving; in this environment, taking up a generous initiative is too shocking. The response is the very notion of distributive justice: what decides it is the dignity of the action as such. Even if the failure is all too predictable, this consideration cannot be relinquished. Moreover, the forgetting of giving is not what is predominant.

Decentralization

If a entrepreneur invests with risk, one cannot say that he is rich—or poor—. On the other hand, the entrepreneur who demands Keynesian conditions is rich; but an active entrepreneur, who accepts the consequences of the primacy of supply over demand, is a man of means, but one who knows how to use them, and so the more means he has the better for all. From this point of view, certain guilt complexes are not justified and should be rejected. The entrepreneur, who is sometimes surrounded by critiques of capitalism, feels that he is without moral support: just confusion. With regard to the entrepreneur who is only half so, or a quarter so, who calls for a guaranteed demand, it is possible to make a morally negative qualification; but it is better to say that, strictly speaking, he is not a entrepreneur. Moreover, these situations are understandable and are not new, because they depend largely on the past, on customs or ways of doing things that create a state of opinion. What can be taken away from all this is a project: it involves going from Keynes to Say, a task that in many professional circles, not only businesses, is long and can be made difficult because of several factors.

In order to carry this project forward, it is fitting that there be a periodic renewal of managerial positions in businesses. The economic process is empirically conditioned by technology. Adaptation to technical changes makes the generational renewal of businesses advisable, because those who, by virtue of the division of labor, are specialized in one technological model do not understand the next one, and a chance has to be given to others. Even if technology were to stay constant, such a revitalization would be desirable so as to avoid the decadence that is peculiar to the governing class. Moreover, the continued success of one type of economic supply consolidates a stereotyped demand. In my view, what is most useful about the ideal of competition is the renewal of businesses. Competition within an established or static system is a struggle concerning the market. But if competition means being replaced by the next generation, by younger people with greater capacity for struggle and more enthusiasm, then the market is renewed. Such a replacement does not entail the ruin of the old businessmen; it is, simply, a reshuffling of the governing minority. It is also true that the turnover of businessmen must be done quickly in countries with a high level of technology, which does not seem to be compatible with large businesses. Large businesses are usually determined by outdated techniques and are bureaucratic. Bureaucracy is an issue not only for the State. In the West, and due to the influence of Keynes's approach, three major forms of bureaucracy have developed over the last few decades: state bureaucracy, union bureaucracy, and business bureaucracy. A policy of decentralization is needed in these three institutions. That monstrosity that is the Leviathan State has given all that it can; there are no longer any countries capable of putting up with such a State. But unions have also become bureaucracies that are currently in crisis; the big unions also require decentralization because, as I have already stated, the differences due to the specialization of work have become more pronounced. An all-encompassing union is a centralism that is justified only by big business. But decentralization is good for businesses too, precisely because they would otherwise be unfit for competition in time. Big businesses are very cumbersome and changing them is difficult; they adapt poorly to critical junctures and in their moments of crisis they require subsidies if massive unemployment is to be avoided. If big business continues being the backbone of the economy, then the future closes up. Disengaging from it requires the renewal of entrepreneurs.

The business centers of California, Florida, and Texas (the three states that have taken the reins of the United States' economy) and the Italians are creating small businesses, or rather, a horizontal coordination (something like a federal structure) that also represents a high degree of decentralization. Even multinationals, considered by some as an extreme case of capitalist gigantism, are already discovering their fondness for decentralization. Another problem that bureaucracy poses is the difference between the moment that an order is issued and the moment of execution. In large administrations this difference increases and compromises the timeliness of the order. It must at least be conceded that information technology mitigates this problem.

The individualization of responsibility also contributes to decentralization. The present day theory of costs developed in Germany aims to calculate it analytically. The idea is to assign to each agent, and in the least amount of time, the cost that his way of acting represents. To the extent that this is achieved, the workers are "motivated", they are made to see the importance of their behavior in the common task. No matter how productive and giving we human beings may be, there is always another side to every human work. Since man is not God, all human work involves some cost, and it is very interesting to not attribute it to the agents in general, but rather to each one. This is another way of decentralizing. To take a simple example, one can specify how much a pilot who delays take off costs an air travel company. It is certainly good to know this because, if there is competition, a company that is not very serious about the departures of its flights loses money. From this point of view, no mode of conduct is indifferent. The supply capacity of all the social agents needs to grow. To do this, it is necessary that each one know their responsibilities. A society of free men cannot be based on ignorance of one's own cost, something that leads to demoralization. This is another aspect of what an economy based on supply might mean, one in which it cannot be said that there are rich or poor, because it allows for the expansion of those characteristics that we saw in the family.

Organizing the division of labor in a correct way on a level that is superior to the family requires a connective. As I have already stated, the connective is normally identified with trade, because it is clear that division of labor is not possible without trade.

But trade alone does not ensure social cooperation to a sufficient degree. At the same time, the elimination of the separation between rich and poor cannot be done solely on the basis of the notion of equality or commutative justice. Strictly speaking, equality is not a human objective. To postulate that either we all make the same amount of progress (which is impossible) and move toward equality, or that no one has the right to make progress, is, as Nietzsche says, to base society on envy; whoever is not envious prefers the difference, as long as it does not give rise to division or to selfish atomism.

If we were to focus only on trade and if we were to entrust everything to the ideal of commutative justice, then we would be moving within a utopian or unreal order and, by resorting to forced procedures that quickly reveal their ineffectiveness, we would waver back and forth without ever leaving the framework. In the first place, by ignoring the supplying nature of the entrepreneur's activity, we would be adopting the position that rejects the primacy of supply and hands it over to demand, which is equivalent to arbitrating an extrinsic remedy to the entrepreneur's supposed resignation in the face of risk. The socialist interpretation of Keynes takes advantage of his appraisal of demand in order to reaffirm their conviction that what is most important is redistribution: taking from one pocket to fill another, because historic socialism becomes uneasy when someone has more than another. Socialists of late have been partially abandoning Keynes. The PSOE* itself considers that socialist Keynesianism is not very practical—in spite of the statist and centralist obsession of European socialism—because it is now already clear that without business initiatives it is not possible to escape from the impasse. This means accepting the Keynes of the activation of supply, which is the most classical one and is concerned about a situation of depression. But since, on the other hand, economic statism is not abandoned (which implies budget deficits) and since increasing demand would provoke high inflation (which leads to a monetary policy of a liberal type), the aforementioned waver-

---

* Editor's note: PSOE stands for "Partido Socialista Obrero Español", the Spanish Socialist Worker's Party

ing would become a jumble, an incoherent mixture that demoralizes the social agents.

In the face of all this, I propose that the entrepreneur should take it upon himself to reject the validity of Keynes's diagnosis. If he does not, he discredits himself as a entrepreneur. How are jobs created? By setting up businesses. Are businesses set up with a guaranteed demand, or not? If with a guaranteed demand, then Keynesianism; if not, then supply with risk. The entrepreneur who, within prudent limits, accepts risk seems preferable to me even if it were only for aesthetic reasons. Moreover, working with assured demand is illusory in an undeveloped country, and when it is possible it gives rise to a consumer society; that is, to the exaggeration of material needs to the detriment of the spirit.

From the point of view of a pragmatic socialist, the consumer society is a perfect ideal: without the need to eliminate the market and to have recourse to central planning (in a Sovietical way), it is already possible to administer abundance, and it is possible to present a type of socialism that is distinct from Marxism. But the consumer society belongs to the past. So, it is not just a question of aesthetics. From the point of view of a promoter, to live without risk is to live like an old person; an old man cannot take many risks because he knows that he cannot face them. In contrast, state protectionism is contrary what being an entrepreneur really means. It is not only a question of details, because the difference within the order of practical consequences is very large. To opt for free business, but with the demand guaranteed, is a kind of mixture that contains a sophistic mistake. It is what is understood by some as the social economy of the market. From the point of view of the entrepreneur, social means that the demand is guaranteed. From the point of view of the social-democratic politician, it is the justification for state bureaucracy; and from the unions' perspective, it is a pretext for the representation and defense of workers that it officiously attributes to itself.

The agreement between the major bureaucracies has always seemed artificial to me. If there was not trickery, it would have had results; but there is trickery: precisely shared bureaucraticism. During the era when big businesses were solid and stable pillars of industrial society, Keynesianism had a possible empirical (non-theoretical) functional justification. But the inadequacies of a deficient approach were bound to appear. We cannot continue to follow a vision that was valid in the 1950s and 60s (perhaps, by inertia, in the 70s); at present, in the United States there are several million businesses that have been created after those decades, which have nothing to do with conventional American corporate gigantism. In Europe the grand solution seemed to be for businessmen to sit down at the same table to dialogue with union leaders and politicians. In this dialogue, unions play the role of guaranteeing the increase of demand. The unions take credit for success in increasing salaries; that is, the increase in purchasing power: they claim that these are their achievements. This is a trick card, because this is the function that corresponds to them according to Keynes's approach. The entrepreneur, in accordance with a narrow economic rationality, proposes what the salary increase could be, that is, the degree of security in the demand that eliminates risk: ultimately, the entrepreneur is in agreement with the unions (homogenous productive series are guaranteed: another trick). Here, we are no longer speaking about class struggle, but rather of economic and social cooperation. The State ensures the terms of this agreement with its tax system, its protectionism, etc. (it justifies itself as bureaucracy: the trick continues). This is how Belgium, for example, has functioned.

Today, Belgium is one of the European countries whose organization is most problematic, among other things, because this formula rests entirely on big business whose guarantors are, at the same time, its parasites. For this reason, the setup is very rigid, and is thrown into disarray as soon as marginal considerations make themselves felt. Nevertheless, Belgium is situated in what the theory of economic spaces calls the center, which in Europe is the axis of the Rhine, extended to Milan, in Italy, and with an attempted branch up to Lyon, in France. Ever since England was incorporated into the common market, its economy has descended toward the south of the island. In Italy, the border of the mezzogiorno has risen from Naples to Rome[6]. If one takes North America as the center, then South America would be a market that is always depressed. On the other hand, the increasing importance of the southwest United States opens up interesting prospects for northern Mexico. Another important space is the Pacific Ocean.

In any case the focus can no longer be big business. Information technology can accentuate the deconcentration and modify the so-called theory of economic spaces, because the movement and exchange of information is different from that of physical goods. But today centralized gigantism is very strong in the production of news, the dissemination of which is carried out by the so-called mass media. This denomination is expressive: the information that is received from newspapers or from television is excessively homogenous, skewed by the influence of obtuse ideologies and without formative value because of its emotional charge which inhibits the intellect. It is, in sum, a superficial and sophistic offering, an indoctrination for a worn out consumerism, the last card of the providential State.

The real entrepreneur puts supply before demand. If this is so, then the Keynesian model is not criticized: it is simply abandoned, because the way to ensure continued investment comes with the definition of the entrepreneur. There is no discussion about whether or to what extent demand effects supply, or if horded savings needs to be distinguished from productive savings, or if it is better to emphasize that the savings rate is compromised by excessive demand (consumption). The rejection of large bureaucracies is due to the fact that decentralization is consistent with authentic business conduct.

---

[6] This theory of economic spaces is debatable. A new formulation consistent with telematics is relevant for the future of the Iberian peninsula; perhaps also for South America.

Observations concerning banks follow the same reasoning. I do not question banks as such; I point out that the banks have joined the Keynesian game and have wanted to be arbiters of the situation; that is, they have practiced a selective credit policy that does not favor permanent investment. The continuity of investment requires generational change. If banks were attentive to this and did not unfairly extend credit in favor of already established businesses (large or small), then they would be serving supply with risk better. The mistakes that banks made by lending to Latin America are not due to risk, but rather to a miscalculation induced by the increase in deposits (petrodollars) and a corresponding economic contraction. The Keynesian model was thought to be exportable. In the end it was discovered that the demand of that continent was inelastic: thus, domestic markets were not created. Without a domestic market, Keynesianism collapses and loans lead to uncontrollable debt. For their part, debtors made the mistake of relying on the exportation of raw materials as a procedure for payment, and by using credit on works of infrastructure they neglected the agricultural sector and provoked a massive movement of population to the cities without corresponding job offers.

The diagnosis is this: a shortage of supply, underutilization of human capacity, population dislocation. Banks reacted to failure by raising the interest rate, a very special offer that is a way of attracting capital; this led to a strong dollar. The sum of these two facts make the repayment of loans more difficult, while at the same time the value of raw materials and of oil drops and North American protectionism reappears. The truth is that these calculations (supply and demand controlled by the value of money; acceptable inflation rates; limits to state intervention, budgetary balance, etc.) move within the parameters that I have described; they are more or less debatable questions of economic science, the legitimacy of which is not being denied. What I am trying to highlight is that economic activity is proper to man; that is, that the anthropological assumptions of economics need to be studied, lest we invent a figure of *homo oeconomicus* that is separated from human integrity, postulated ad hoc, or in accordance with the limits of the method of a "science".

Stimulating demand in an artificial manner leads to a consumerist society; focusing development with this goal in mind is humanly devastating. On the other hand, creating supply means controlling demand; if production depends on assured demand, then the major processes are channeled toward baubles and the economy is turned into a trivial human activity. It is illusory to try to establish social peace on the basis of the demoralization of man, on the transformation of the citizen into a consumer. Likewise, putting entrepreneurship at the service of consumption like a line that can be extended without end undermines the role of business. Business cannot accept this game—it has to give up this type of gain. If underdevelopment is a consequence of weak supply, then the omission of distributive justice by the country's ruling minority has to be denounced.

The attempt to imitate big business is an anachronism. The Americans have assimilated the lesson. Even before Reagan, they had already put into motion an extensive process of setting up small or mid-sized businesses. These businesses naturally ran into a problem of credit, but they figured out how to solve this through a type of credit initiative, invented on the fly, that puts savings in direct relation with the subjects of business supply. The market problems that these businesses encounter are due to their limited advertising capability. The great focus on advertising that persists in advertising shows itself to be inconsistent with the new business organization. The difficulty is overcome by a diminution of the homogeneity of the market, something that makes possible a control of the demand that, because it is plural, places a limit on the consumer society.

As I have already stated, by following after demand, supply is capricious and becomes trivial (returning to the family model, it would be as if a father attended to the child's every whim). I have also said that consumerism is a consequence of the functions that the unions attribute to itself (precisely because there is no sufficient integration of its members in the business it-self). The substitution of big centralized businesses lessens the need for union control.

Communication

The division of labor, as a set of different activities, requires a connection that, for the moment, is trade. Trade is, indeed, indispensable (if the baker cannot exchange his bread for something else, why specialize in making bread?). But, as I have pointed out, it is not true that everything takes place on this level. At the same time, it does not seem to me that the ideal of equality is justified; nor, indeed, is the difference be-tween poor and rich understood as correlation. Nevertheless, if one focuses only on trade, this difference cannot be avoided. Now, the division of labor is presided over by another connec-tion that is discovered whenever one accepts that supply comes before demand or that society is possible only if man gives before receiving.

In my view, this is what justifies being an entrepreneur. The function is not only economic. The provider of the family that I mentioned is also an entrepreneur, as well as the professor who dares to go beyond the limits of a conventional program, or the inventor, or the parish priest who offers the Good News. In general, whoever assumes risk is an entrepreneur, as long as the risk is run when giving something. For this same reason, it seems to me that a worker, if he is well integrated into the business and not simply protected by the union, is an entrepreneur. The cost analysis that I mentioned is a way to encourage good business behavior. Understanding man as someone who offers before being a receiver is consistent with his character as person. The person reinforces the exchange of goods from above. The economic sciences should not disre-gard this fact, not even for reasons of methodology, because economics does not exist without personal relationships. But there is yet another connective of the division of labor that can be called basic. This connective is inherent to technical know-how, that is, to human making that transforms matter. What is most characteristic of technical instruments is that they constitute a plexus. An isolated instrument is impossible—it is not an instrument at all. An instrument always points to another. The man's practical activity produces means, and the means are useful if there are other ones. The means are always *intermediates*—means among themselves—because they are destined to a superior end that cannot be other than man (and, through man, God). Everything that man makes has a medial value because the character of end corresponds to the person. It is evident that it is what is intermediate that sustains trade.

If what is produced by some people did not have a medial interconnection with what others produce, then the division of labor would be absurd; even more, man would not work. Human production is characterized, precisely, by interdependence; therefore, the division of labor is a differentiation, but not a rupture, because all the things that man makes refer to each other.

Making hammers makes no sense if nails are not also made, because the hammer is for nailing; but the nail and the hammer do not make sense if there is nothing to nail: pieces of wood in order to make a table, for example. A table, in turn, makes no sense if it is not useful for something. What is characteristic of a means is that it is useful. Nothing is useful by itself; rather, it is useful in connection with that for which it is useful. Human culture is the ordering of a number of means, which, because they are such, require one another. Following Heidegger, I call the connections of things that are capable of use the total plexus (*Ganzheit*). Whoever does not know what a means is useful for does not understand its *being* a means. The understanding of a means lies in its use. If one does not know how to use it, the means is reduced to something for show.

It can also be put like this: the means are means if they are available, and if they are not known as available, then they are not known as means nor are they available. Insofar as they are available, the means are can be organized, and the corresponding mode of being in man is his practical conduct. Organized practical conduct without a relationship to means is not possible, because practical conduct on the human level organizes means and is organized by means. That is why, the division of labor is possible—above all, by the way of being of the means, and not primarily by trade, since trade also presupposes it. If what one does not connect by reference to what another does, then there is no trade. Nor would the supply be effective.

I will attempt to briefly describe the relationship between supply and means. The understanding of the means is *formal*, that is, the means are understood according to the *form* of using them (nails are nailed with the point, and not the other way around) precisely because the means are originally rational human contributions: being contributed points to the person's offering. For this reason, the understanding of the means is not initially social (but rather a type of monopoly). Now, since the means enter into the plexus that supports the division of labor, the understanding of it expands. For this reason, it is correct to say that civil society is constituted to the same extent that several human beings understand the means that form a plexus. If a person does not understand, or does not know how to use, he excludes himself, or is excluded, from the social relationships that are constituted by this complex. Civil society therefore requires participation in the supplying, something that is communicated. Communication is the general social connective that makes the means understandable in their connection.

The structure of the means (referring to each other, and being known only as such) clearly points to a typical configuration that is language. The means par excellence is the word. Every connection between material instruments is a case, a particularization, to which language can be applied. Just as money is the means that makes the generalization of trade possible, language is the general connective of the medial plexuses insofar as they are comprehensible. This is the primary meaning of the Greek word hermeneutics, which is usually translated as interpretation. Hermeneutics, in Greek, does not exactly mean that; instead it means that articulation of reason according to which a thing is understood by another: it is not understood in itself, but rather insofar as this thing refers to another. This way of understanding is indispensable for practical reason. Therefore, it would be the same to say that the means constitute a plexus, as it is to say that the being of the means is hermeneutic.

Information technology's value for the strengthening of a new society that is more human lies in its capacity to improve the communication and the comprehension of practical relationships.

The foregoing considerations open up an interesting question: knowledge is an integrating factor of social life; consequently, we have to ask if this factor can increase its influence in a not too distant future. Indeed, Western civilization clearly demonstrates the project of linking its historical dynamic with increase in knowledge. This project has taken an institutional form: universities and other specialized centers are dedicated to the cultivation of knowledge and to research. Their achievements are widely disseminated through a multifaceted work of publishing. Perhaps the situation is mature enough to be oriented toward a general intertwining of knowledge and work.

Knowledge and Work

It is frequently said that a new society is at hand. And even that the transition toward it has already begun, in such a way that our present is unstable or changing because the models that have prevailed until now resist disappearing and, at the same time, are fracturing, are showing themselves to be incapable of lasting. Some call the new society postindustrial; other authors talk of the society of knowledge. Both terms are meant to refer to the same thing. Accordingly, the postindustrial society would be the society of knowledge.

If one accepts that knowledge is the highest dimension of the being human, the supreme form of life—and this is the classic thesis—, then the society of knowledge would be a supremely

42

perfect society. Strictly speaking, society is advanced by human energies and thus constitutes a space in which the fruits of these energies condense, flow back over human beings, and embrace new generations. This involves a two-way flow according to which men make society and society situates its members. Consequently, the concept of the society of knowledge is multifaceted, and its meaning has to be declared by answering the following questions: In which institutions is knowledge socialized? With which instruments is it more clearly incorporated? How is knowledge integrated into human action? How does it determine social relationships? The first question refers to the University and to centers of research. The second formulates the question of so-called artificial intelligence. The third points to the connection between knowledge and work. The fourth concerns itself with organization, with the configuring presence of knowledge in social relationships and with the important theme of decision[7].

Although the answer to the questions posed involve considerable difficulties, I want to insist on the advantages that in principle a society of knowledge implies with respect to other social forms. In my view, this advantage lies fundamentally in making human work dignified. The more human work has to do with knowledge, and the more cognitive elements are inserted into and configure the productive activities, the more it is humanized and the more it is freed from its materialist burden, and the more the essence of the economy and its progressive character is developed, since the economy advances to the extent that it draws closer to and conforms itself to the nature of man.

Historical Interpretations of Work

As I see it, the great advantage that the society of knowledge brings is this: the elevation of economic activity to a sufficiently human level, something that can only be achieved to the

---

[7] Some observations regarding these questions are formulated in the previous section.

extent that the higher dimensions of man form part of economic activity. If they do not form part of it, then the system of production is a mere support for the expansion of the life that remains closed to it. Let us recall, for example, how the Greeks conceived the relationships between human perfecting and work, what the structure of the *polis* was in the Classical perspective.

For Aristotle strictly productive activities are proper of slaves. The slave is not defined as a mistreated being, but rather as that being who, strictly speaking, is not human because he is not capable of perfecting himself. The slave is a human being that is in a state of constant immaturity, stuck in a level of humanity that he cannot overcome. Economic activities belong to the slave. Not to the freeman, because he must dedicate himself to what perfects him, and we have agreed that the pure satisfaction of basic necessities does not perfect man at all.

Human perfecting is extra-economic. Everything that man is capable of attaining in his life—human teleology—is overflowing with respect to the pure provisioning of constant necessities; precisely for this reason it is extra-economic: it is neither work nor connected with work. This is so to the point that, as historians of that period have noted, it is not that the Greeks did not have the technical skill, especially in the Alexandrian period, or that they could not make progress in this field. What happened is that they did not want to; for them it was not a project for the future. The incorporation of more knowledge into work did not interest them. Knowledge was a self-sufficient reality; the direction of life belonged to it, but insofar as human life is spiritual. Thus, in Plato the distinction between the sensible and rational levels becomes almost a rupture, which Aristotle seeks to heal on the constitutional plane: but he always remains on the operational level. Human spirituality has nothing to do with work.

This approach has gradually changed. The clearest change of the classical approach is what is called the industrial revolution. However, this change contains an imbalance within it.

The imbalance of capitalism consists of the following: the previous approach has changed, because, otherwise, the increase in productive activity is impossible. The exclusion of what is spiritual-human from economics is now no longer complete: because economic activity is now no longer merely material activity carried out by slaves, who are imperfect and non-perfectible human beings; although the situation has dramatically changed, economics is nevertheless conceived by a large portion of economic agents as an activity with no spiritual relevance.

There is a clear imbalance in capitalism; when it erupts, the contradictions of which Daniel Bell speaks appear. This imbalance can simply be described like this: capitalization, accumulating capital, is an activity of a spiritual nature. One cannot capitalize without an elevated ethos, without a moral guide, so much so that capitalization is done according to the model for acquiring virtues. Capitalization is a form of feedback, an increase in the starting point, that is, a teleologization, a growth. The basis of the progressive economy, which is capitalization, is akin to the spiritual, and, nevertheless, its unfolding, that is, the productive economic process, is not. From this, two human types arise: ethical beings, who are the capitalists; and non-ethical beings, who are the economic agents. That they are non-ethical means: external to ethics, which means nothing but the impossibility of perfecting themselves in their activity. This can of course lead to an accusation, which is exclusively ideological and the product of a poorly planned and poorly formulated moral indignation. The truth is that in an industrial society work is purely repetitive.

Industrial society, to the extent that it culminates in its own terms, demoralizes everyone because it seeks the solution to its imbalance in mass consumption; and mass consumption is the logical consequence of human imperfection. Which is more imperfect: working in an assembly line, or stuffing oneself with trivialities during free time? It's all the same.

Thus, there is a fundamental error unless a materialist anthropology is accepted. Greek anthropology is not materialist. What happens is that it distinguishes the material from the spiritual, and does not properly unite them within the dynamic order. But an industrial society distinguishes what within it is valuable from what happens in the great production chain planned in a Taylorian manner in which each one does what they are supposed to do at each moment, but knows nothing of the overall product because it involves partial and automatic activities; and the proof of this is that man can be replaced by a robot, thus fulfilling Aristotle's observation that if workshops were to function by themselves, slaves would not be needed.

The Crisis of the Industrial Society

This is the industrial society in a nutshell. I insist on the imbalance that is proper to it. This imbalance has given rise to contradictions; that is, it has led to a culture (which in this situation is more radical than work) that contains a negation of work and dissociates itself from all ethics: a culture of the mass man that is a subculture, a counter-culture or a culture of immediacy. A culture of pure immediacy, of "I like this or I don't like this", is the degradation of culture. A truly remarkable rupture has been produced. The result is that culture becomes disengaged from work. On the other hand, there is a problem of the allocation of resources that the economic system cannot resolve; it involves achieving a situation of widespread well-being that needs to be administered from an instance that is distinct from the economy. The welfare state thus appears, and politics becomes disengaged and enters into conflict with economic rationality. The situation cannot be worse, although since we are still very much in it, it seems normal to us. A correction to this development is contained in the previous sections.

It seems to me impossible to extract a high level anthropology from the functioning of an industrial society. On the other hand, the society of knowledge—understood as a society in which the human ingredients that form part of social functioning are better—makes it possible to maintain that the human being cannot be reduced to the situation of mere animality.

This is a great opportunity (problems are more like opportunities, as psychologists say). We begin to be in a position not so much to change man—the essence of man—, but rather to change the human meaning of the economy, to move toward an economic model whose exemplar cause, whose paradigm, is man himself. On the other hand, attaching importance to the economy is justified only to the degree that this is achieved. The economy cannot have any prestige if it is like what the Greeks said it is, or if it is as unbalanced as it is in the industrial society. And the Marxist objection is useless, because the work value is merely a postulate (the same is true of the equivalence of theory and praxis) if the spiritual is relegated to the condition of a superstructure. Work has value if it integrates human elements at the highest level; otherwise, it is the machine that possesses more value. Unless man *can handle* the machine; that is, unless the amount of humanity exercised when using it is greater than the amount of humanity that has been employed to do it, work is nothing more than technology. If it is not more than technology, but less, then the idea of the value of work is not the key to progress.

The Social Institutionalization of Knowledge

Let us say a few words concerning the social status of knowledge. Insofar as knowledge has to do with subjects, it is possible to compare teaching and research with the activities that readers carry out in a library.

To illustrate the problem that this poses, I will make use of a text from Borges, which is quite ironic. It is a text that speaks of a library in which all knowledge is contained. The unfortunate thing about this library is that it is impractical; the library exists, but it cannot be managed, precisely because it is infinite. Everything is there, but can man know all of it? Thus, this library raises a problem of adequacy, because it appears that it is not a library built to human scale. If it was not built to the scale of the individual intelligence, perhaps some type of collective procedure could facilitate measuring up to this library. And this is the social organization of knowledge: if one individual cannot do it, then it is only through the community of readers that the existing mass of knowledge can be assimilated by the human being. Now, if it cannot be covered by one individual, then this will have to be done in the form of a division of intellectual labor. Which means, in turn, that it is possible to form—starting with its study by segments—a synthesis, a duplicate learned from the library. However, what is characteristic of the library is that, based on how it is managed, it does not give us its own criterion of organization, since the volumes within it appear to be gathered together according to some extrinsic criteria, and it is not guaranteed, nor is there anyone capable of figuring out, if there is a system of knowledge that corresponds or fits well with the shelf organization by which the library is presented to the reader. There is a certain cumulative character that does not guarantee the organization or the internal structure. For this reason, the library taken in its totality is Babel, that is, chaotic. There is no guarantee that the knowledge obtained from it is unified; we do not know its value as a system (using the word "system" in a purely indicative way) because, from the practical point of view, we are incapable of unifying the objective content of the library, since we cannot manage it in its entirety.

By having recourse to the social organization of knowledge the same question is raised once again. We find ourselves faced with a situation that is a bit strange, one of perplexity. Are we capable of being faithful to the deep structure of the library? And what structure would we use if we know it only in part or by parts? This is the problem of specializations. We know more and more, but it is more and more specialized and the characterizations that are attempted hide a fragmentation that leads to atomization. The taxonomy itself becomes practically useless; it does not provide a good criterion for coordination, but is limited to reflecting the dispersion.

It is clear that the transition to a society of knowledge is impossible if the problem of the division of knowledge is not faced. Specialized knowledge is incapable of dealing with what is often called complexity. We are in a complex age in which everything depends on everything (complexity means interdependence). But if what is complex is approached from the point of view of specializations, then it is seen only in parts, and this means that it becomes ungovernable. This is one of our present day's determining factors, which can be described in the following way: the confluence of separate inspirations—incommunicable because of specializations—produces an uncoordinated dynamic conjunction and gives rise to so-called perverse (contrary to what is intended) effects and results that are null. From this flows a discouraged and insecure psychological temper.

If every problem should be seen as an opportunity, then the one that we are now considering leads to an undertaking that is interdisciplinary. Only interdisciplinary knowledge makes it possible that the hope for a society of knowledge is a real, certain hope, and not a project that only results in new frustrations.

The interdisciplinary motto is a modality of the complementarity between competition and collaboration that José María Basagoiti referred to. It is not a question of a vague proposal, or of a new illusion. I will try to show its exact meaning by establishing the following thesis: there can be no true theoretical knowledge, or practical knowledge without reference. Both theory as well as practice *are annulled if they fall into self-reference*, that is, if they tautologically refer back to the same thing (to themselves). I will illustrate the thesis with some examples. First of all, this is verified, as I said, on the instrumental plane: a hammer refers to a nail, not to itself. To use a hammer is to hammer something else. The hetero-reference is constitutive of what is called means. A self-referred means is neither a means nor is it known as such. The references between the means constitute a plexus, a totality of relationships.

Another example: on page 154 of the Spanish edition of a curious book titled *El vendedor al minuto* [*The One Minute Salesperson*] it says: "People do not work for anyone except for themselves." This sentence can be understood in two ways: self-referentially, the phrase destroys itself, since it means the negation of the person (who is substituted by a mere *himself*). It is an expression of selfishness. But the sentence can be understood in a hetero-referential sense: the person works for herself insofar as work perfects her. The person is the end of the action that she executes, insofar as action ennobles her. Work is hetero-referential in the order of means, both because its result enters into a plexus, and because it is a perfective personal act of the agent.

The same must be said of voluntary acts. Indeed, if knowledge were self-referential, reflexively closed, then the will would be impossible, because the will is preceded by the intelligence and the acts of the will constitutively point to the other. On the social plane, special importance is given to orders, which are acts of decision that refer to others. In the industrial society, the knowledge of managers deals directly with production and, as a function of this, deals with the organization of work. Correlatively, the managers' decisions use the knowledge that they avail of for adjusting production to market information. This means that the worker does not participate in this latest information, and is therefore ignorant of the motives that drive the managers' decisions. The greatest difficulty of this peculiar isolation consists in that both the worker as well as the decisions of the managers function in real time, which can be affected by the aforementioned isolation. One of the opportunities that a society of knowledge offers to businesses is the disappearance of this anomaly. Working with knowledge brings the decisions of the economic agents closer to the management level.

Books by Leonardo Polo

Complete works in Spanish

Obras Completas de Leonardo Polo, Serie A, Vol. I-XXVII, Eunsa, Pamplona 2015-present

English Translations of Polo's Works

1. *Ethics. A Modern Version of Its Classic Themes.* (Sinag-Tala Publishers, Manila 2008)
2. *Why a Transcendental Anthropology?* (Leonardo Polo Institute of Philosophy Press, South Bend 2014)
3. "Human Feelings" in the *Journal of Polian Studies* (2014)
4. "Friendship in Aristotle" in the *Journal of Polian Studies* (2015)
5. "University Professor" in *The European Conservative* (Winter/Spring 2016)
6. "On the Origin of Man: Hominization and Humanization", in the *Journal of Polian Studies* (2016)

www.ingramcontent.com/pod-product-compliance
Lightning Source LLC
Chambersburg PA
CBHW021221020426
42331CB00003B/411